THE HEART OF SERVING LIKE A PRIEST

'SERVING MANUAL'

BY RUTHANN JOHNSON

Copyright © 2025 Ruthann Johnson

All Rights Reserved. No part of this book may be used or reproduced by any means, graphic, electronic, or mechanical, including photocopying, recording, taping, or by any information storage retrieval system without the written permission of the publisher except in the case of brief quotations embodied in critical articles and reviews.

Unless otherwise identified, Scripture quotations are taken from the King James Version (KJV).

Scripture quotations marked AMP are taken from the Amplified Bible copyright © 2015 by The Lockman Foundation, La Habra, CA 90631. All rights reserved.

Scripture quotations marked AMPC are taken from the Amplified Bible, Classic Edition. Copyright © 1954, 1958, 1962, 1964, 1965, 1987 by The Lockman Foundation. All rights reserved.

Scripture quotations marked EASY are taken from the EasyEnglish Bible Copyright © MissionAssist 2019 - Charitable Incorporated Organisation 1162807. Used by permission. All rights reserved.

Scripture quotations marked TLB are taken from the Living Bible copyright © 1971 by Tyndale House Foundation. Used by permission of Tyndale House Publishers Inc., Carol Stream, Illinois 60188. All rights reserved.

Scripture quotations marked NLT are taken from the Holy Bible, New Living Translation, copyright © 1996, 2004, 2015 by Tyndale House Foundation. Used by permission of Tyndale House Publishers, Inc., Carol Stream, Illinois 60188. All rights reserved.

Scripture quotations marked TPT are from The Passion Translation®. Copyright © 2017, 2018, 2020 by Passion & Fire Ministries, Inc. Used by permission. All rights reserved.

THE HEART OF
SERVING LIKE A PRIEST

TABLE OF CONTENT

Prologue	vi
Priestly Oath	1
Where should I start?	5
Organigram	17
Standard Operating Procedures	27
Priest of Baal vs Priest of God	29
Serving Accountability Challenge	33

PROLOGUE

This manual is designed to be the practical supplement to the theoretical lessons shared in the book, "When Kings Rule and Priest Sacrifice." It deals with the fundamentals of serving and serves as a guide to help the believer identify the potential areas they can serve in and how to serve effectively.

PRIESTLY OATH

It's a solemn promise, often invoking a divine witness, regarding one's future action or behavior; that's what an oath is.

Cultivating the right heart posture before serving.

"And indeed it was not without the taking of an oath [that Christ was made priest] (for those Levites who formerly became priests [received their office] without [its being confirmed by the taking of] an oath, but this One [was designated] with an oath through the One who said to Him, "The Lord has sworn And will not change H is mind or regret it, 'You (Christ) are a Priest forever '"). [Ps 110:4]" - Hebrews 7:20-21 AMP

As you embark on this exciting journey of commitment to serving in the house of the Lord, my prayer is that you'll begin with a sense of reverence and awareness, understanding that your service is unto the Lord.

Christ is our ultimate example; he is indeed our High Priest. He was unwavering in His commitment to serving, and so should we, in that our commitment should extend beyond the confines of a building and circumvent the restricted times allotted for corporate gatherings.

We are priests forever, which means that our private and public lives should reflect that of our royal heritage. We must endeavor to align our lives in a way where our conduct always reflects Christ. This is what we are committing to, not just helping at church but subjecting ourselves to a life of accountability and fellowship where iron truly sharpens irons, and the countenance of one brightens the other.

ARE YOU WILLING TO?

- Abandon every form of evil, deceit, hypocrisy, feelings of jealousy, and slander for the sake of promoting unity and teamwork as you serve. - **1 Peter 2:1 TPT**

- Be done with every trace of wickedness (depravity, malignity) and all deceit and insincerity (pretense, hypocrisy) and grudges (envy, jealousy) and slander and evil speaking of every kind to give no place to the devil and cause the work of the Lord to be hindered. - **1 Peter 2:1 AMPC**

- Be obedient to those who are assigned to lead your team/ministry/department, having respect for them and eager concern to please them, in singleness of motive and with all your heart, as [service] to Christ [Himself]– Not in the way of eye-service [as if they were watching you] and only to please men, but as servants (slaves) of Christ, doing the will of God heartily and with your whole soul. - **Ephesians 6:5-6 AMPC**

- Serve the Lord by serving alongside your team/department/ministry with reverent awe and worshipful fear, not casually or haphazardly, but with intentionality - **Psalm 2:11 AMPC**

WHERE SHOULD I START?

Start with your personality or gifts test.
GO AHEAD...

This section gives you an overview of the results of a few personality tests so that you can learn about different personality types and choose the test you'd like to complete to discover your uniqueness and how to serve your team effectively. Here are some tips to consider as you complete your personality test:

- Find a quiet time to complete it and give it your undivided attention.
- Be honest - answer the questions based on what you most likely do, not what's ideal or what you aspire to be or do.
- Take your time, what's the rush?

"So encourage each other to build each other up, just as you are already doing." - 1 Thessalonians 5:12 TLB

HOW CAN WE EFFECTIVELY ENCOURAGE EACH OTHER IF WE KNOW NOTHING ABOUT EACH OTHER? LET'S START WITH THE BASICS . . .

TELL US ABOUT YOURSELF

First and Last name:
_____

Birthday: Anniversary (if any):
_____

Love language:
_____

Favorite color:
_____

What are your talents? Tell us what you're good at:
_____

_____

_____

Hobbies/Interest:
_____

_____

_____

Career field:
_____

_____

PERSONALITY TYPES

Here's a list of personality types for us to review and do the corresponding personality test so we can better understand each other:

MARC ACETTA PERSONALITY TEST:

"Once you learn how to read people's colors (Red, Blue, Green, Yellow) you will have a competitive advantage in understanding what will be the most effective way to communicate with them."[1]

- **Blue:**[2] Fun-loving, bright, spontaneous, and generally jovial, 'blue' people are the type that "lives for the moment." They are extremely sociable and outgoing and like to be out in the sun. They prefer to follow strong leadership and are willing to cooperate as long as they get treated nicely. On the downside, they tend to be forgetful and are usually not mindful of their time. Due to their spontaneity, they are impulsive buyers and as a result, spend their money freely.

- **Green:** People in this category are rational and calculated thinkers. They try to research exhaustively before deciding on something and refrain from making rash decisions. They are natural cynics and are usually skeptical of other people's motives; probably because they do not trust their intuition as much as facts. As a result, they are very realistic and they possess a proclivity toward prejudging people. They

---

[1] https://marcaccetta.com/personality-test/
[2] http://marc-accetta.blogspot.com/2012/12/interpreting-colors-unveiling.html

are also systematic and pedantic, sometimes necessitating guidelines by which they can abide. They are also notorious for being emotionally detached.

- **Red:** Confident, challenge-oriented, competitive—these are probably the three most appropriate adjectives to describe 'red' individuals. They tend to hang out with fellow achievers, despite their many insecurities and their strong desire for approval. They are also known for being good decision-makers. On the other hand, they can be short with people and prefer to be in the VIP section. This does not make them particularly good team players.

- **Yellow:** Easily the most personable among the four types, 'yellow' types are extremely loyal and are very good team players. They value honesty and integrity and are very family-oriented. This is largely the reason why they prefer to follow ethical leaders. They love all forms of life and are very environmentally conscious, thus making them great outdoors people. They try to avoid conflicts and confrontations as much as possible and usually take on the role of a peacemaker in dire situations. They love to support charities and other worthy causes, thus impelling them to dislike greedy and materialistic people. They are also creative, expressive, and unpretentious.

ENNEAGRAM TEST:

"Enneagram[3] is one of the most powerful and insightful tools for understanding ourselves and others."

1. THE REFORMER
The Rational, Idealistic Type: Principled, Purposeful, Self-Controlled, and Perfectionistic.

2. THE HELPER
The Caring, Interpersonal Type: Demonstrative, Generous, People-Pleasing, and Possessive.

3. THE ACHIEVER
The Success-Oriented, Pragmatic Type: Adaptive, Excelling, Driven, and Image-Conscious.

4. THE INDIVIDUALIST
The Sensitive, Withdrawn Type: Expressive, Dramatic, Self-Absorbed, and Temperamental

5. THE INVESTIGATOR
The Intense, Cerebral Type: Perceptive, Innovative, Secretive, and Isolated.

6. THE LOYALIST
The Committed, Security-Oriented Type: Engaging, Responsible, Anxious, and Suspicious.

---

[3] https://www.enneagraminstitute.com/type-descriptions/

7. THE ENTHUSIAST
The Busy, Fun-Loving Type: Spontaneous, Versatile, Distractible, and Scattered.

8. THE CHALLENGER
The Powerful, Dominating Type: Self-confident, Decisive, Willful, and Confrontational.

9. THE PEACEMAKER
The Easygoing, Self-Effacing Type: Receptive, Reassuring, Agreeable, and Complacent.

GIFTS TEST:

"As a follower of Jesus, exploring and exercising your spiritual gifting is a vital and exciting part of your spiritual journey. This test is designed as a tool to help you discern the spiritual gifts God has given you."[4] Each gift is a divine strength and ability to do a task effectively.

- **Administration** - to organize multiple tasks and groups of people to accomplish these tasks.

- **Craftsmanship** - to plan, build, and work with your hands in construction environments to accomplish multiple ministry applications.

- **Exhortation** - to strengthen, comfort, or urge others to action through the written or spoken word and Biblical truth.

- **Helps** - to work in a supportive role for the accomplishment of tasks in Christian ministry with the ability to often see the need before others do.

- **Hospitality** - to create warm, welcoming environments for others in places such as your home, office, or church.

- **Intercession** - to stand in the gap in prayer for someone, something, or someplace, believing for profound results.

- **Service** - to do small or great tasks in working for the overall good of the body of Christ.

---

[4] https://giftstest.com

THE 5 LOVE LANGUAGES TEST:

"It's a simple and effective way to identify how you receive love to strengthen your connections so you can experience greater joy and harmony in all of your relationships as you serve."[5]

- **Acts of Service** - For these people, actions speak louder than words. Laziness, broken commitments, and making more work for them tell speakers of this language their feelings don't matter.

- **Quality Time** - This language is all about giving the other person your undivided attention. Distractions, postponed dates, or the failure to listen can be especially hurtful. Quality Time also means sharing quality conversation and quality activities.

- **Words of Affirmation** - This language uses words to affirm other people. Actions don't always speak louder than words. Kind, encouraging, and positive words are truly life-giving.

- **Physical Touch** - Hugs, pats on the back, and thoughtful touches on the shoulder can all be ways to show excitement, concern, care, and love. To this person, nothing speaks more appreciation than appropriate physical touch.

- **Receiving Gifts** - For some people, receiving a heartfelt gift is what makes them feel most loved. Don't mistake this love language for materialism; the receiver of gifts thrives on the love, thoughtfulness, and effort behind the gift.

[5] https://5lovelanguages.com/

16 PERSONALITIES TEST:

"Learn what really drives, inspires, and worries different personality types,[6] helping you build more meaningful relationships."

1. **Architect** - Imaginative and strategic thinkers, with a plan for everything.

2. **Logician** - Innovative inventors with an unquenchable thirst for knowledge.

3. **Commander** - Bold, imaginative, and strong-willed leaders, always finding a way – or making one.

4. **Debater** - Smart and curious thinkers who cannot resist an intellectual challenge.

5. **Advocate** - Quiet and mystical, yet very inspiring and tireless idealists.

6. **Mediator** - Poetic, kind, and altruistic people, always eager to help a good cause.

7. **Protagonist** - Charismatic and inspiring leaders, able to mesmerize their listeners.

8. **Campaigner** - Enthusiastic, creative, and sociable free spirits, who can always find a reason to smile.

---

[6] https://www.16personalities.com/personality-types

9. **Logistician** - Practical and fact-minded individuals, whose reliability cannot be doubted.

10. **Defender** - Very dedicated and warm protectors, always ready to defend their loved ones.

11. **Executive** - Excellent administrators, unsurpassed at managing things – or people.

12. **Consul** - Extraordinarily caring, social, and popular people, always eager to help.

13. **Virtuoso** - Bold and practical experimenters, masters of all kinds of tools.

14. **Adventurer** - Flexible and charming artist, always ready to explore and experience something new.

15. **Entrepreneur** - Smart, energetic, and very perceptive people, who truly enjoy living on the edge.

16. **Entertainer** - Spontaneous, energetic, and enthusiastic people – life is never boring around them.

Which personality test was the most significant to you?

What's your personality type?

List the 'pros' or 'strengths' of your personality type:

List the 'cons' that you'll be working on as you serve:

ORGANIGRAM

An organigram is an organizational diagram used to help volunteers understand the church's organizational structure. It identifies key roles and responsibilities and helps to improve communication since teams will know exactly what department is assigned to resolve their concerns.

"Come, all of you who are gifted craftsmen. Construct everything that the Lord has commanded:' - Exodus 35:10 NLT

"And He has filled him with the Spirit of God, with ability and wisdom, with intelligence and understanding, and with knowledge and all craftsmanship," - Exodus 35:31 AMPC

'The Lord has filled him with his Spirit so that he has special skills. He knows how to make many kinds of things." - Exodus 35:31 EASY

WHAT SPECIAL SKILL HAS GOD GIVEN YOU?

Organizing departments within the ministry helps to improve efficiency by allowing volunteers to specialize based on their area of expertise or giftings. It also creates accountability and allows the building of deeper bonds as they interact with like-minded members of their teams.

Organizations use it to improve efficiency. If a local church were to adopt that same blueprint to help organize its volunteers and become more effective, here's an example of what that would look like.

1. HUMAN RESOURCE DEPARTMENT

They are responsible for overseeing the people. They manage serving-related tasks and engage the team. This may involve recruiting volunteers, creating a rewards system, and addressing any issues or concerns.

They play a vital role in the overall success of a ministry by attracting, developing, and retaining volunteers and by creating a positive and productive serving environment.

Teams/Roles within HRD:
- **Onboarding** - Introduce new volunteers to the ministry (history, culture, organizational structure, core values, list of areas to potentially serve in, etc)

- **Training and Development** - Design and deliver training programs to enhance the team's skills, giftings, knowledge, and effectiveness in the area they serve.

- **Compensation and Benefits** - Create a rewards or recognition system for volunteers to encourage, appreciate, and motivate them to continue in their commitment to the work.

- **Performance and Compliance Management** - Create and communicate Standard Operating Procedures (SOP) for volunteers, set expectations, conduct regular evaluations, and make recommendations for assignment rotation when volunteers aren't able to effectively execute the assignment they've been given.

- **Volunteer/Employee Relations** - Handle concerns, resolve conflicts, manage disciplinary actions, and promote unity among the team.

2. ADMINISTRATIVE DEPARTMENT

They are responsible for the daily operations of the ministry. They manage the facilities, supplies, and equipment; schedule meetings; act as a liaison for ministry requests; manage the church calendar; as well as other administrative and clerical tasks.

Teams/Roles within Admin:
- **Secretarial** - Maintain physical and digital filing systems; schedule meetings; update church calendar, etc.

- **Communications** - Handle emails, letters, and phone calls; and relay information between departments and members.

- **Travel Laision** - book travel and accommodations for ministry-related events (in-house, locally, or internationally), liaise between guest speakers and the appropriate teams to provide adequate support during events both in-house and externally.

3. FINANCE DEPARTMENT

The Pastoral and Executive teams rely on the knowledge and hard work of the finance department to help them make informed financial choices and effectively steward the church's financial resources. They are responsible for ensuring that the church's financial operations are conducted in a legal, efficient, and effective manner; they monitor revenue, expenses, and debt.

Teams/Roles within Finance:
- **Accounting** - Prepare financial statements, forecasting cash flow, manage budgets, and developing financial strategies. They also play a key role in helping them make important financial decisions, such as where to invest their resources, how to raise funds, and how to manage risk.

- **Procurement** - Oversee spending to ensure that departments comply with the budget and to determine whether certain programs need changes in funding; determine the necessity of a request and its level of urgency; provide the most cost-effective resolution; and keep abreast with the current inventory/assets thus reducing wastage.

4. CUSTOMER SERVICE DEPARTMENT

This is the first impression guests get when they visit the church. They are responsible for making everyone feel welcome, handling complaints, and providing information about the ministry.

<u>Teams/Roles within CSD:</u>

- **Hospitality** - Ensure that members or guests have a positive experience with the ministry. They arrange seating, provide refreshments, and are the initial point of contact during services.

- **Retention** - They provide proactive outreach by creating or implementing systems that allow the ministry to effectively follow up with its guests and plug them into the right programs, be it discipleship or membership.

5. INFORMATION TECHNOLOGY DEPARTMENT

The IT department is assigned to manage and maintain the church's computer systems, networks, and software applications.

<u>Teams/Roles within IT:</u>

- **Technical Support** - They ensure that the church's IT systems are secure and protected from unauthorized access, provide technical support to volunteers, and many more.

- **Broadcast** - Their primary role is to ensure that the organization's technology resources are utilized efficiently, securely, and in line with the church's goals and objectives to spread the gospel. They manage and maintain the church's website, online presence, and all outlets used to broadcast the messages.

6. PRODUCTION DEPARTMENT

They are responsible for overseeing the entire service or event from project conception to actualization. They provide the framework for services or events to be conducted in decency and order.

Teams/Roles within Production:
- **Creative Arts** - The creative team that uses dance, music, songs, etc, during a worship service to formulate a beautiful orchestra that welcomes the presence of the Lord and invites the congregation to bask in His glory.

- **Media Production Team** - Capture footage and manage all on-set audio as dictated by the director based on the vision of the house and what needs to be broadcast. Unlike the IT department, their main responsibilities encompass what happens during a worship service. They play a key role in ensuring that divine encounters are captured, digitally documented, and accessible for future reference.

- **Production Design** - They're responsible for the overall aesthetic of the facility during worship services or events. They ensure that every visual element aligns with the vision or theme, including the decor, dress code, signs, invitations, etc. They also coordinate with the appropriate departments to acquire equipment (if needed) and organize the logistics for events.

7. OPERATIONS DEPARTMENT

They manage the day-to-day activities that are required to run the ministry. This can include managing and coordinating the use of resources such as labor and equipment.

Teams/Roles within Operations:
- **Ministerial** - This represents the fivefold ministry or those who serve the body through intercession, exhortation, counseling, or even help non-Christians take the necessary steps to become born-again Christians, etc.

- **Safety/Security** - Provide security and train appropriate teams on safety procedures.

- **Facilities Management** - Coordinate maintenance and repairs of the church facilities. Promote a safe environment by identifying potential hazards, and implementing safety protocols.

- **Compliance** - Ensure adherence to administrative policies and procedures as well as applicable laws and regulations.

CALL TO ACTION

WHAT SPECIAL SKILL HAS GOD GIVEN YOU?

WHICH DEPARTMENT WOULD YOU CONSIDER SERVING IN?

STANDARD OPERATING PROCEDURES

When a new volunteer starts serving, there is little chance of success if no clear goals or behavioral boundaries are clearly set in place for them. Without clear goals, positive outcomes become unlikely.

For this to happen, the leader has to lay the foundation for the team. This means setting defined boundaries, leading by example, and creating a clear path for each volunteer to navigate. To achieve common goals, clearly defining the culture of the ministry with the volunteers is a necessity.

EXCELLENCE

As a king and priest, the same standard of excellence that we function with corporately is the same way we serve within these areas:

- Punctuality
- Accountability
- Dress code and professionalism
- Personal hygiene

CULTURE

- Be professional, dependable, and courteous at all times.
- Respect all Team Members and you will be respected as well
- Work safely and look out for your teammate's well-being.
- Learn as much as you can from as many as you can - and make use of it.
- Communicate promptly and clearly with all your teammates.
- Serve with honesty and integrity at all times.
- Be proud of your work; you're making a significant impact in the kingdom of God.

PRIEST OF BAAL VS PRIEST OF GOD

As believers, we're all being perfected in one way or another, as such, here's a list of protocols that may be implemented to help us safeguard each other and prevent us from putting ourselves in situations that could cause our character to be questioned or tempt us to compromise our integrity.

We cannot ignore the reality that many have been victims of abuse; we saw it with Eli's sons:

> "Now Eli was very old, but he was aware of what his sons were doing to the people of Israel. He knew, for instance, that his sons were seducing the young women who assisted at the entrance of the Tabernacle." - **1 Samuel 2:22 NLT**

SO HERE'S A RULE OF THUMB. IN SERVING, WE SHOULD NEVER ALLOW OURSELVES TO PARTICIPATE IN ANYTHING THAT VIOLATES THE PRINCIPLES FOUND IN THE WORD OF GOD:

- **Never serve out of fear, manipulation, or compulsion.**

"Moses said to the people, 'Do not be afraid. God has come to test you. He wants you to respect him and to obey him. Then you will not do things that are wrong." - Exodus 20:20 EASY

- **Never agree to do anything that destroys someone else's life or character.**

"You must not murder anyone." - Exodus 20:13 - EASY

- **Never participate in any form of sexual immorality.**

"You must not commit adultery." - Exodus 20:14 NLT

- **Never participate in any form of dishonest or illegal activity.**

"'You shall not steal [secretly, openly, fraudulently, or through carelessness]. [Prov 11:1; 16:8; 21:6; 22:16; Jer 17:11; Mal 3:8]" - Exodus 20:15 AMP

- **Never falsify information to promote any agenda.**

"'You shall not testify falsely [that is, lie, withhold, or manipulate the truth] against your neighbor (any person). [Ex 23:1; Prov 19:9; 24:28]" - Exodus 20:16 AMP

When in doubt, consult the Word of God. Abiding by God's principles will protect us from being victims of deception and corruption. A code of conduct is especially necessary for new believers or the spiritually naive who are still learning to exercise discernment.

ARE YOU READY TO START SERVING?

LET'S TRACK YOUR COMMITMENT

SERVING ACCOUNTABILITY CHALLENGE

Team leaders can use it as a performance assessment to evaluate the team to help identify growth opportunities, potential recipients for rewards, and whether or not a teammate needs to be rotated to another department that would better develop or benefit from that person's skill set.

However, individuals may use this sheet to help hold themselves accountable and track their progress. It is said that it takes 21 days to replace or break a habit, so by committing to it, participants are allowing themselves to cultivate a certain level of consistency and discipline that will help them become even more effective in other areas of their lives.

EVALUATION

Below is a sample evaluation form. This can be done monthly, quarterly, yearly, or as often as the department deems necessary.

SERVING EVALUATION

DEPARTMENT:

Name:

BE-Beginning (I need practice) AP-Approaching (I could use practice) ME-Meeting (I can do it!) EX-Exceeding (I am a Master!)

Criteria	BE	AP	ME	EX
QUALITY OF WORK: Work is completed accurately (few or no errors), effectively and within deadlines with minimal supervision.	☐	☐	☐	☐
ATTENDANCE AND PUNCTUALITY: Reports to serve on time, provides advance notice of need for absence.	☐	☐	☐	☐
RELIABILITY AND DEPENDABILITY: Consistently serves at a high level; manages time and workload effectively to meet responsibilities.	☐	☐	☐	☐
COMMUNICATION SKILLS: Written and oral communications are clear, organized, and effective; listens and comprehends well.	☐	☐	☐	☐
JUDGEMENT AND DECISION MAKING: Makes thoughtful, well-reasoned decisions, exercises good judgment, resourcefulness, and creativity in problem-solving.	☐	☐	☐	☐
INITIATIVE AND FLEXIBILITY: Demonstrates initiative; often seeking out additional responsibility; identifies problems and solutions; thrives on new challenges and adjust to unexpected changes.	☐	☐	☐	☐
COOPERATION AND TEAMWORK: Respectful of teammates when serving and makes valuable contributions to help the team achieve goals.	☐	☐	☐	☐

SERVING EVALUATION

DEPARTMENT:

Name:

BE-Beginning (I need practice)   AP-Approaching (I could use practice)   ME-Meeting (I can do it!)   EX-Exceeding (I am a Master!)

Criteria	BE	AP	ME	EX
QUALITY OF WORK: Work is completed accurately (few or no errors), effectively and within deadlines with minimal supervision.	☐	☐	☐	☐
ATTENDANCE AND PUNCTUALITY: Reports to serve on time, provides advance notice of need for absence.	☐	☐	☐	☐
RELIABILITY AND DEPENDABILITY: Consistently serves at a high level; manages time and workload effectively to meet responsibilities.	☐	☐	☐	☐
COMMUNICATION SKILLS: Written and oral communications are clear, organized, and effective; listens and comprehends well.	☐	☐	☐	☐
JUDGEMENT AND DECISION MAKING: Makes thoughtful, well-reasoned decisions, exercises good judgment, resourcefulness, and creativity in problem-solving.	☐	☐	☐	☐
INITIATIVE AND FLEXIBILITY: Demonstrates initiative; often seeking out additional responsibility; identifies problems and solutions; thrives on new challenges and adjust to unexpected changes.	☐	☐	☐	☐
COOPERATION AND TEAMWORK: Respectful of teammates when serving and makes valuable contributions to help the team achieve goals.	☐	☐	☐	☐

SERVING EVALUATION

DEPARTMENT:

Name:

BE-Beginning (I need practice)   AP-Approaching (I could use practice)   ME-Meeting (I can do it!)   EX-Exceeding (I am a Master!)

QUALITY OF WORK:
Work is completed accurately (few or no errors), effectively and within deadlines with minimal supervision.

BE ☐ AP ☐ ME ☐ EX ☐

ATTENDANCE AND PUNCTUALITY:
Reports to serve on time, provides advance notice of need for absence.

BE ☐ AP ☐ ME ☐ EX ☐

RELIABILITY AND DEPENDABILITY:
Consistently serves at a high level; manages time and workload effectively to meet responsibilities.

BE ☐ AP ☐ ME ☐ EX ☐

COMMUNICATION SKILLS:
Written and oral communications are clear, organized, and effective; listens and comprehends well.

BE ☐ AP ☐ ME ☐ EX ☐

JUDGEMENT AND DECISION MAKING:
Makes thoughtful, well-reasoned decisions, exercises good judgment, resourcefulness, and creativity in problem-solving.

BE ☐ AP ☐ ME ☐ EX ☐

INITIATIVE AND FLEXIBILITY:
Demonstrates initiative; often seeking out additional responsibility; identifies problems and solutions; thrives on new challenges and adjust to unexpected changes.

BE ☐ AP ☐ ME ☐ EX ☐

COOPERATION AND TEAMWORK:
Respectful of teammates when serving and makes valuable contributions to help the team achieve goals.

BE ☐ AP ☐ ME ☐ EX ☐

SERVING EVALUATION

DEPARTMENT:

Name:

BE-Beginning (I need practice)   AP-Approaching (I could use practice)   ME-Meeting (I can do it!)   EX-Exceeding (I am a Master!)

Criteria	BE	AP	ME	EX
QUALITY OF WORK: Work is completed accurately (few or no errors), effectively and within deadlines with minimal supervision.	☐	☐	☐	☐
ATTENDANCE AND PUNCTUALITY: Reports to serve on time, provides advance notice of need for absence.	☐	☐	☐	☐
RELIABILITY AND DEPENDABILITY: Consistently serves at a high level; manages time and workload effectively to meet responsibilities.	☐	☐	☐	☐
COMMUNICATION SKILLS: Written and oral communications are clear, organized, and effective; listens and comprehends well.	☐	☐	☐	☐
JUDGEMENT AND DECISION MAKING: Makes thoughtful, well-reasoned decisions, exercises good judgment, resourcefulness, and creativity in problem-solving.	☐	☐	☐	☐
INITIATIVE AND FLEXIBILITY: Demonstrates initiative; often seeking out additional responsibility; identifies problems and solutions; thrives on new challenges and adjust to unexpected changes.	☐	☐	☐	☐
COOPERATION AND TEAMWORK: Respectful of teammates when serving and makes valuable contributions to help the team achieve goals.	☐	☐	☐	☐

ABOUT THE AUTHOR

Ruthann Johnson is a gem whose life is committed to advancing the kingdom of God. She's a strategist who is constantly seeking ways of becoming more effective.

OTHER BOOKS

Ruthann has also written:
- **The Art of Transition** - learn to experience maximum productivity in what seems to be the most difficult seasons of your life.
- **Pride ain't Prejudice** - learn about overcoming childhood trauma and being a standard bearer who lives a life of sexual purity to the glory of God.
- **When Kings Rule and Priest Sacrifice** - learn about the power of serving in your local church.

Introduce children to the Bible, excitingly and interactively, with her collection of **Puzzle Books**! Designed for young and teenage learners, these books are filled with fun word search puzzles that help kids engage with God's Word while improving their vocabulary and problem-solving skills.

WORDSEARCH PUZZLES:
- Jehovah
- Great Kings
- Prophets
- Judges
- Proverbs 31 Women
- The Armor of God
- Biblical Numerology

CROSSWORD PUZZLES:
- The Parables of Jesus
- Miracles of Jesus
- The Mind of Christ
- The Disciples of Jesus
- The Gifts of the Spirit
- The Fruit of the Spirit
- Five-fold Ministry

MAZES:
- Joshua - Road to Prosperity
- Jericho Walls
- The Red Sea
- Walking on Water
- Elijah by the Brook
- Abraham on the Mountain
- Jesus at the Well

LOVED READING THIS BOOK?

GIVE IT AWAY!

If reading this book has impacted your life and you would like to order more copies for those in your sphere of influence (perhaps your church, small group, company, friends, or family), please don't hesitate to get in touch with us to get a discount on a bulk order at: ruthann.c@icloud.com.

OTHER PROJECTS

Ruthann has also served the body in other capacities:
- **Open Pockets** - A Finance Podcast where she shares biblical principles to empower listeners to become better stewards of their finances. It's aired Thursdays [bi-weekly] on several podcast platforms.
- **CHRISTIANE** - A clothing line that specializes in clothing alterations infused with scriptures from the Word of God, with some designs being hand-stitched beaded work.

For more information on any of these products or services, please don't hesitate to get in touch with us at: ruthann.c@icloud.com. You can also view her link-tree page @ruthannchristiane for the latest updates.

www.ingramcontent.com/pod-product-compliance
Lightning Source LLC
Chambersburg PA
CBHW081330040426
42453CB00013B/2371